The Perils and Pitfalls of Horse Ownership

– A tongue-in-cheek guide

Written and illustrated by
Johanna Sharpe

The Perils and Pitfalls of Horse Ownership

– A tongue-in-cheek guide

Written and illustrated by
Johanna Sharpe

The Perils and Pitfalls of Horse Ownership

A Callisto Green Publication

ISBN 978-1-909985-13-1

First published in 2016 by
Callisto Green
4 Caprice Close
Swindon
SN5 5TB

www.callistogreen.com

A copy of the CIP entry for this book is available from the British Library.

To my mother Anne Farncombe, without whom I wouldn't have had gained my introduction and passion for the equine world, or access to those penciles and endless sheets of white to transfer my thoughts to paper throughout my childhood.

Introduction

The Perils & Pitfalls of Horse Ownership – A tongue-in-cheek Guide documents many of the essential blunders which have often been made by horsey folk when they are at the less experienced end of the scale.

As the owner of the Rein and Shine Equestrian Centre, I have spent much of my time teaching people to ride, training horses, and observing horse owner's special brand of behaviour when it comes to their favourite horse. I try to highlight the humour of the small things in the equine world, which horse lovers of course can blow out of all proportion, such as the way keeping a horse warm at night can turn into sheer frivolity of ceremony, with many horse owners adorning their horses beyond normal measures, to the point where the horse has more clothing and a comfier bed than they do!

The oversensitive nature of horses is something I have always enjoyed cartooning; a paper bag, for example, can become a demon when caught by the wind, and a cross-country fence a place off utter terror! Yet to a human, these appear to be normal and everyday objects. The wiring of a horse's brain can be a minefield; they so often have become misunderstood creatures and labelled as 'naughty' or 'too flighty', when at times the real problem is the fact that they have been mixed with the inexperienced horse handler!

For many people, the 'joy' of learning to ride can be the fondest of their horsey memories. I will always remember leaving the arena in floods of tears as a child when scolded for not holding my hands in the 'correct' position! The overbearing instructor's words have never left me! At the time, this was an event which nearly put me off riding, but as I look back now, I can laugh at myself and the tyrannical teacher. (Although cunningly, I have added her to the book as an advert for bad instructors!)

The idea behind *The Perils & Pitfalls of Horse Ownership* has always been for us to be able to laugh at ourselves – I have been the subject of many of these illustrations over the years, poking fun at my own inexperience when I was at the point of buying my first horse and loaning my first pony, and I now see others treading the same path I did all those years ago. I like to explore through my work (now that I know) what the horse is really feeling and thinking, and conveying this with as many human qualities as possible so the reader can understand what the world is like looking at it through the horse's eyes.

The first twelve months of owning a horse are considered to be the hardest months of all. This is where you really learn that the outside appearance of glamour attached to the equine world is really just that – an appearance! The smallest part of owning a horse is the riding; the rest is simply navigating through a battle of wills between the horse and the owner. Many new owners give up in this time, finding the commitment too hard for almost no reward. As the book unfolds, it is clear that horses can run rings around us in very funny scenarios, but it also shows that sticking with it does bring the reward – and this is the real message behind the humour.

I hope that many horse fans and horse owners will be able to relate the pages to their own experiences, and see themselves or someone they know in the pages, and like I have done, perhaps look back and have the opportunity to laugh at those treasured moments we all took so seriously at the time.

Buying your First Horse

So you're finally ready to buy your first horse!

This is the most exciting phase of horse ownership, dreaming of that one special creature who will be your trusted friend, and show off your horsemanship skills so that everyone around you can see what an amazing understanding of horses you really do have.

You long for that once-in-a-lifetime creature who will look after you and understand you and your style of riding.

You want to find a horse who is beautiful and talented, easy to ride and ready to bring home the ribbons at every competition.

Your friends will be in awe as you parade your skills before them on your prancing palomino princess!

HORSE SALES

So where do you buy a horse?

There are two purchase options for buyers: the route of the Horse Dealer or that of the Private Seller.

Unfortunately, both paths can be difficult to navigate. Taking someone with you who is experienced in these matters is a very good idea.

Many horses bought at dealerships have had one lady owner with low mileage, have never broken down and have excellent body condition!

Buyers need to be aware that without any accurate previous history available it is always a lottery once you have gone ahead with the purchase.

When buying from a private seller, you usually have a better understanding of what previous experience the horse has acquired.

Good sellers will often allow a short trial period before purchase which allows buyers to get to know their new horse a little.

Buyers need to
be careful with
private sellers as they
can become blind to
their horse's dangerous
behaviours, branding them
as 'little quirks' and often
creating a sale price from
their heart instead of current
market values!

DIY Yard
£10 pw

Home, sweet home

Your new horse is going to need somewhere
comfortable to live which suits both of your needs.

If you don't own your own property, you will need
to look for a Livery Yard.

There are many yards which cater for a 'do-it-yourself' livery option and assisted service options. It is always wise to have a look around and consider your options.

First-time horse owners must not be blinded by cheap horse accomodation only to later find themselves in a dangerous environment.

On the other hand, you might consider a full livery option, where your new steed is looked after for you with his every need catered for.

Some upper-end establishments offer five-star facilities in wonderful settings...which also comes with a five-star price tag!

With livery yards, you get what you pay for!

GRANGE LIVERY

Once you have decided on the perfect horse, it is wise to get him vetted with a clean bill of health by a local vet before you complete on any sale.

The check-up

Most owners will insure their horses against injury at the very least; the last thing you want is a large veterinary bill if your horse becomes unwell. The insurance company will need a copy of the vetting certificate.

The vet will expect your horse to jump through all sorts of hoops to thoroughly check him out!

Transportation

With the sale agreed and the vetting passed, your new best friend will need transportation arranged to his new home.

This can be a very stressful experience for all concerned, but is usually a very exciting experience too.

If you are lucky, your new horse will load first time. Those who are not so fortunate can spend hours persuading their horse that the trailer is not a monster.

Be prepared to have a friend on standby for assistance!

Always remember to be calm and follow safe practice; encouragement through force is not recommended!

Isolatation

Most yards will insist on a period of isolation for
your new horse in the interest of disease prevention.

New horses always present
a risk to others and so
a period of isolation will
follow for up to two weeks.

During this time it is
advisable that you give your
horse something to do to
help him pass the time
without too much stress,
such as grazing in hand
or long periods of fuss and
grooming.

Some horses can go stir
crazy in isolation and try
every method possible to
make a break for freedom!

Introductions

Following the period of isolation, the new light of your life will now be able to be introduced to his new herd!

This is always an interesting day and usually very entertaining. As you look on nervously, your new prince will be strutting his stuff, showing off the range of his movement to the onlooking, bewildered herd.

You will now spend an eternity trying to get him to recreate such movement when you ride him!

Early Days

Horses thrive on routine and a stable environment. Changes should be made slowly and carefully.

You will now need to support your lifelong friend by giving him the consistency he will need to settle into his new home.

The mantra of all first-time horse owners should be: stability, stability, stability...

...just don't get confused with the type of stability you should be offering!

Your first ride!

The day has finally arrived when you are able to have your first ride at the new yard!

This is always an experience to be remembered, as horses can often take months to settle in before their true characters are revealed and can often be on their toes a little at first.

On the plus side, you may experience views of the countryside you might not otherwise have seen, so investing in some good safety gear for riding is a very sensible idea!

You may be surprised at just how willing your new best friend will be!

After all the leading around you have given him, it is only right that he might want to return the favour!

Preparing your horse for the competition season

The next step will be getting your new horse fit for the competition season, which will provide the two of you with some good focus to your work.

Lunging your new best friend is a good start on the road to getting to know each other and will help with his fitness.

You may need to brush up on your lunging technique as first-time horse owners do not always have a polished technique!

There will be some good days and some challenging days with your new horse. It is important not to give up at the first hurdle and develop a good deal of perseverance.

Horses test our patience and confidence. To improve, we must stay the course.

Asking for help

Asking your new horsey friends for help can be a wise move when facing difficulties with your steed.

Their years of experience can be utilised for free, giving you the benefit of their knowledge and wisdom.

Just make sure you choose carefully who you ask for advice from; many horse owners will be self-confessed equine masters!

They can overdo their so-called helping hand, often taking the inexperienced into their 'management'!

Settling Down

Once your new best friend starts to settle in, his personality may change. He will become more relaxed about his surroundings and start taking life in his stride.

Taking time out to enjoy any positive experience is essential.

Your horse may surprise you from time to time and begin to look after you for a change as the bond between you begins to grow.

The busy life you have saddled yourself with can be very demanding. Your work will still need your full commitment, yet your mind will always be elsewhere.

Your bank balance will suffer too as the yard claims more and more of your work clothes!

There will come a time when you start to find your feet, navigating your way through the horse world and starting to take pride in the little things.

Be careful of the amount of time you spend preening your stable...someone may be feeling a little left out!

Balancing Acts

The 'worries' is a condition all new owners will suffer from and it never really goes away. You will worry about your horse's health, his stable, his feed, his tack...the list is endless.

Whilst it is healthy to be aware of your new steed's welfare, you must be careful not to overdo it.

Try and find time to focus on the other parts of your life too.

Partners can feel left out in the cold when your horse begins to take top priority!

On the up-side, if your friend moves in, you'll have more time to catch up with the soaps!

Training and

Competitions

Finding the right instructor to bring out the best in your relationship with your new pal will be very important.

GOSSIP 100

Instructors can vary. There are those who can train horses, those who can train people, and those with the gift to train both.

Never choose anyone who will make you feel worthless and small. An instructor's role is to encourage achievement, rather than beat it out of you!

47

Your first competition

The exciting day has finally arrived when you are ready for your first competition. After all of the hard work you have put into your new horse's fitness, you are expecting greatness from him!

Everyone gets nervous and worried about their horse's behaviour, let alone parking the lorry!

Whilst it is important for your horse to look his best, just be careful not to overdo the plaiting!

Equipment

You will see many other horse owners at your yard using different pieces of equipment on their horses.

Some of these owners are experienced horse people and understand complicated tack and devices.

Sadly, in every yard there is a portion of owners who will copy these people.

Remember, horses are as individual as you and I, so be careful not to fall into the copycat trap. All the gear and no idea is not a good look!

Repetition, repetition, repetition

Training your horse will be a lifelong pursuit. You will continually need to reinforce his confidence through repetition of task.

Do remember that groundwork with poles and small fences will need much practice.

Not every horse is a natural athlete!

Showjumping

After all those bruises, hard work and dedication, you are now ready to enter your first showjumping class!

You have been dreaming of that triumphant feeling as you wave your red rosette not so discreetly under the noses of everyone at your yard. Finally you can show the world how good the two of you can be!

Just remember that your jumping partner may not feel the same way that you do!

Cross-country

It is important to continually develop your skills with a variety of activities.

This is just as essential for your new horse as it is for you, in order to prevent boredom with the same activity.

Cross-country schooling is great for improving both athleticism and jumping skills.

If your horse is new to cross-country fences, it may be wise to invest in a sturdy neck strap!

Hunting

There is simply no end to the new pursuits you and your horse can take part in to broaden your horizons.

You will need to be well prepared for your first time hunting. Many horses enjoy running with the group and learn not to react to the hounds barking around them, and all horses must be fit enough to cope with the changing terrain and conditions.

It is advisable to prepare for a soaking, especially if your horse is not a fan of water!

Behaviour

Many new owners notice that their beloved angel starts piling on the pounds and begins to exhibit lively and erratic behaviour.

Guilt feeding is usually at the heart of the problem. Perhaps you were late to fetch in (so you gave him a little extra feed) or you felt sorry for him when he ran out of hay (so you gave him a little extra feed).

Before you know it, you will have passers-by wondering when his baby is due!

During the course of your journey with your new horse, your patience will be pushed to its limits. Horses by nature will push their boundaries constantly. As the leader in your double act, you will need to stay in charge.

Grooming

As the seasons change, so will your trusted steed. In the autumn you will notice your sleek beautiful friend turns into a fluff ball. Do not be alarmed; he is just growing his new winter coat ready to cope with the colder conditions coming.

This can be quite an ordeal for your washing machine as your clothing emits horse hair on a massive scale.

To cope with the hair, this is the time that many
owners will clip their horse's coat. This will mean
that they are able to keep on working thorough the
winter without losing condition by overheating in
their winter coats, and then getting a chill.

The art of clipping is not something at which first-time horse owners always excel.

Shaving off the coat of their beloved with a large, noisy and heavy set of clippers often fills them with terror and trepidation!

The pressure of creating neat lines, knowing everyone will be looking, watching and judging every move, is often enough to force many into outsourcing the whole thing.

Nothing can prepare a new clipper for the sea of multi-coloured hairs which will now be found in every orifice for weeks to come!

Once your little prince has been clipped, you may consider cutting off (hogging) his mane.

There are reasons for this, such as tidiness or uneven mane growth.

Once you do decide to take the plunge and go the whole hog in your quest to tame unruly hair, do spare a thought for your friend, who may have enjoyed the warmth his mane provided!

If you are lucky, your perfect pal will allow you to remove unsightly leg and facial hair too. Well-behaved horses usually allow an all-over trim without a fuss.

But if you are unlucky, your fuzzy friend may need extensive securing!

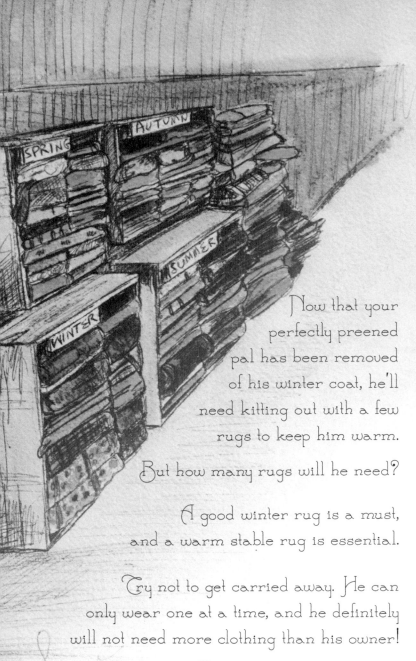

Now that your perfectly preened pal has been removed of his winter coat, he'll need kitting out with a few rugs to keep him warm.

But how many rugs will he need?

A good winter rug is a must, and a warm stable rug is essential.

Try not to get carried away. He can only wear one at a time, and he definitely will not need more clothing than his owner!

Autumn

Reduced grazing time due to wet and muddy fields, along with loss of daylight, can mean that horses spend much longer in their stables at this time of year.

Horses can be full of extra energy which they need to burn off at any opportunity.

You may find that every blade of grass suddenly represents a gallop, and open spaces mean you'd better hang on!

The Winter Months

During the winter months you will need to make plans to fit daily routines in around the diminishing light.

You may end up turning out, fetching in and mucking out all in the dark...

It might be wise to invest in a good torch. Finding your horse using your mobile might take you all night!

Your friend's first Christmas

The first Christmas with your horse is always exiting, from opening the horsey gifts which your family will get into the routine of buying you every year, and choosing the special gifts which you will now purchase for your beloved four-legged friend.

Christmas day horsey traditions at yards usually
consist of over-merry groups hacking out in
celebration of the day. Be careful not to get to carried
away in the pre-hack drinks; losing the way would be
a rather embarrassing tale over Christmas dinner!

Grit and determination

On cold mornings it can be difficult to tear yourself away from a warm bed, defrost the car and brave the cold before work to feed and turn out your new horse.

Slipping out in your PJs at 5am to feed and muck out can be hard on those not conditioned to the outdoors lifestyle! Your horse too will find the strange, cold and icy world difficult to navigate. Staying grounded will help you both slip through those tough morning routines!

Settling Down

By this stage, most new horse owners have reached a level of comfortability with their four-legged creature, relaxing into the horsey life and coming and going as they please.

Their new friend is no longer a novelty and the honeymoon is over.

But this is when habits and shortcuts in routines can start to creep in. Owners should be careful not to compromise safety just to save a few minutes in their daily routine!

Many first-time horse owners make the mistake of ceasing to have lessons once they have their own horse, believing that the level has now been reached where they are free to do as they please.

The truth is that the journey has only just begun and it's important to remember that a rider never stops learning, no matter what level they reach. The instructor's time is important, and their advice, energy and knowledge should be utilised as much as possible to keep you on the right track. After all of your hard work and effort, it would be a shame to let bad habits or childish behaviours creep in!

It can be hard to shape up again once you have let routines slip. When it's raining or cold, fair-weather riders will often opt out of coming up to the yard, leaving their precious prince to fend for himself.

Remember that your horse is a lifestyle commitment; he relies and depends on you.

Staying away from the yard or spending less time with your horse will not go unnoticed or unpunished!

Continuing to work on your horse's skills as well as your own is important, especially for your horse, as he will get bored without a varied work routine.

Before you attempt more showjumping competitions, honing your own skills will be invaluable.

Nervous or inexperienced jumpers will often try to lift the horse over the jump, resulting in a nasty jerk of the horse's mouth. Remember that it's your job to deliver him to the fence, and it's his job to jump it!

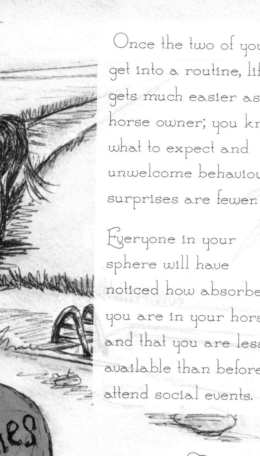

Once the two of you get into a routine, life gets much easier as a horse owner; you know what to expect and unwelcome behavioural surprises are fewer.

Everyone in your sphere will have noticed how absorbed you are in your horse and that you are less available than before to attend social events.

This is a time that can cause friction for those who care about you as they can often feel they have lost you to a horse. Who or what to put second to your horse can be a real conundrum!

After the training and hard work you have put in, there may well be times you do bring home the winning rosette!

These rare times are to be cherished and remembered fondly. When the partnership finally comes together and everything goes well it can be the most fantastic feeling on earth.

Just remember the one who did most of the work before your celebrating begins!

WINNER &

A Lasting Bond

Now at the end of your journey you are now no longer considered a rookie!

Those around you at your yard will believe that you have developed some level of expertise forged by the path you have trodden.

You have survived nearly a whole year of trials and tribulations, and have gained invaluable Experience!

As a result of this, it has finally happened...you have become so bonded with your horse that the two of you are now inseparable!

About the Author

Johanna Sharpe is the owner of Rein & Shine Equestrian Centre in North Wiltshire. She has been cartooning the world of horses since early childhood, bringing drawings to life though her unique style of illustration. Johanna graduated with a BA Hons degree in Art & Media Studies at the University of Hertfordshire in 2003, after completing a City & Guilds in Life Drawing and an Art Foundation degree. Always drawing, she illustrated for her school newspaper and even caricatured her teachers, earning her an award for her comical endeavours.

Johanna has had a lifetime with horses and has spent much time working with very challenging breeds. She has spent many years re-training ex-racehorses and helping them find useful homes after racing careers. Johanna is a BHS-qualified riding teacher, and she still competes and trains her own horses, as well as teaching equestrian studies to special educational needs children at her centre. Running her own business, the British Horse Society Highly Commended Rein & Shine Equestrian Centre with her partner John McDonald, the centre opened in 2013 and brings together the couple's passion for animals and education.

The Perils & Pitfalls of Horse Ownership – A tongue-in-cheek guide is Johanna's first published cartoon book, fuelled by the world around her and the comical elements that occur on a daily basis between horse and rider. Bringing a lifetime of observations and real experiences to paper, the work seeks to show the comedic side of horses and allows the reader into the horsey world from a new perspective.

Acknowledgements

I would like to thank my partner John for his kind support during the creative process. I would also like to thank Lauraine Phelan for her encouragement and supportive friendship, and Calisto Green publishers for believing in the work.

A Callisto Green Publication

Lightning Source UK Ltd.
Milton Keynes UK
UKOW07f0515120416

272067UK00011B/44/P